P9-EMC-643

Homework Solutions For Weary Students & Their Parents

Copyright (c) 2001 Victoria Olivadoti
ISBN: 0-9713302-0-4

All rights reserved. Except as permitted under the Copyright Act of 1976, no part of this book may be reproduced, in any form or by any electronic or mechanical means, including the use of information storage and retrieval systems, without permission in writing from the copyright owner.

Requests should be addressed to:
    Tori Publishing
    10932 El Coco Circle
    Fountain Valley, CA 92708
    Or by Email at homeworksolutions@hotmail.com

Edited by Gerry Kaskel

Designed by Morris Advertising, CA

Also by Victoria Olivadoti:
Homework Solutions for the Weary Parent
Homework- A Guide for the Weary Teacher

Acknowledgements

This book is dedicated to the memory of my father, Richard Matzkin. He was willing to take risks for an idea he believed in deeply. He could willingly face challenges and always saw solutions to problems. He believed life was like a bowl of lemons. He would say, "You can cry that you have sour lemons, or you can make some lemonade."

I'd like to give special thanks to my mother, Phyllis Matzkin, who guided me and supplied the foundation for this book.

I dedicate this book to my niece, Susan Berger, who encouraged me to create a book for students.

With deep appreciation for their support and encouragement, I thank the following people:

I would like to acknowledge my nieces, Emily Hart for embracing the contents of this book and Erin Berger whose helpful suggestions were invaluable. I also want to thank my daughters, Shelly Olivadoti for her terrific artwork and words of encouragement and Melissa Olivadoti for her wisdom. Thank you, Brad and Maria Souder, you are the greatest promoters. Patty Berger, Sande Hart, Marcia Sykes, Jackie Pensa, Karen Hainlen, Anne Morris, Karen Wells, Judy Fleischmann, Mary Reynolds, Alan and Marci Schultz, Elaine Sarkin, Karen Connor-Johnson, Cindy Helliwell, Kim Saunders, Kathy Henderson, Lynn Bogart, Kathy Blake, Aunt Alma, John Sullivan, Sydney Nichols and Corrie Grudin, thank you for your input and constant support. I would also like to thank Gerry Kaskel for her capable editing. Last but not least, I want to thank my students past and present for being the best teachers of all and for providing me with the material found in this book.

Homework Solutions for Weary Students & Their Parents

Written By
Victoria Olivadoti
Illustrated by
Shelly Olivadoti

About the Author
Written by her daughter

Vicki Olivadoti resides in Fountain Valley and is currently teaching in Huntington Beach, California. She also finds time to serve as consultant to school districts, teachers, students and parents. Vicki boasts a 30-year career in which she gained extensive experience in teaching children of varied educational backgrounds, ages and skill levels. She also successfully guided my sister and myself through school using the very tools found in this book. This book and the one that came before it, *Homework Solutions for the Weary Parent*, are a direct result of Vicki's enthusiasm for teaching and her altruistic nature to help others. The "Homework Solutions" series was born from one woman's ability to see a challenge and rise to meet it by finding a solution for parents throughout the nation to help their children become successes in school and in life.

Homework Solutions For Weary Students & Their Parents

Written By
Victoria Olivadoti

Illustrated by
Shelly Olivadoti

Does Homework Give You The Fits?

There are many actions you can take to help yourself. Sometimes all you need to be a better student is a little coaching. As your coach, I'd like you to follow the steps to success:

The 1st Step:

Ask yourself, "What exactly gives me a problem with homework?"

Record your answer here:

_____

Before you can improve, you need to identify what is giving you trouble. Once you know, you can look for ways to solve the problem. On the following pages you will find challenges students face that cause them to be unsuccessful with homework. They may help you identify your challenge.

The 2nd Step:

Circle the challenges you experience.

1. I don't like doing it because it is boring. Go to page 13 for help.

2. I lose papers. Go to page 18 for help.

3. I forget the materials I need to complete the assignment. Go to page 23 for help.

4. I am not performing as well as I think I should. Go to page 26 for help.

5. I do the work, but I forget it at home. Go to page 33 for help.

6. I don't know where to begin, so I avoid doing the work. Go to page 36 for help.

7. I don't always understand the questions or the directions. Go to page 38 for help.

8. I never seem to have enough time to get everything done. Go to page 42 for help.

9. I don't know how to do some of the tasks I have to do to complete the assignment. Go to page 46 for help.

10. I seem to get distracted easily while I am doing my homework. Go to page 48 for help.

11. When I ask for help, the adults say, "You're smart, go figure it out." Go to page 53 for help.

12. I don't seem to remember the concepts I study. Go to page 55 for help.

13. The teacher returns my graded work and says I can do better, but I don't know how. Go to page 57 for help.

14. I think I've written an excellent essay, but I get a lower grade than I expected. Go to page 60 for help.

15. I hate the work, so I rush through it and get a poor grade. Go to page 63 for help.

16. I think I understand the homework, but when I get home I can't remember what to do. Go to page 65 for help.

17. I asked my parents to help me get the materials I need. Now they won't let me do the work myself. Go to page 68 for help.

18. I have to do a group project and my partners never do their fair share. Go to page 70 for help.

19. I have a hard time turning in work that is not perfect. Go to page 73 for help.

20. I can't concentrate at home. Go to page 76 for help.

21. Everyone else in my class can do the work quickly, which makes me feel really dumb. Go to page 78 for help.

22. I don't have a place to study at home. It's too noisy. Go to page 81 for help.

23. I have so many after-school activities that I find it hard to start my homework before 8:00 p.m. Go to page 83 for help.

24. I'm a procrastinator. Go to page 86 for help.

25. I'm told to study, but I don't know how! Go to page 89 for help.

26. I don't study the correct items for tests. Go to page 93 for help.

27. I get easily frustrated and I don't even want to do the work. I just don't care anymore. Go to page 96 for help.

28. My homework takes me three hours. Go to page 100 for help.

29. I don't know how to do research, but I am expected to do a research report. Go to page 102 for help.

30. I don't understand the teacher's directions, but I don't want my classmates to think I am stupid, so I don't ask questions. Go to page 105 for help.

31. I don't see why I should do homework. Go to page 107 for help.

32. I can't do my homework because the teacher didn't give me the worksheet. Go to page 109 for help.

33. I can't do my homework because I forgot my book or assignment at school. Go to page 111 for help.

34. I was supposed to have a parent sign my paper, but she got home after I went to bed, so and I got in trouble. Go to page 113 for help.

35. I have a project due in two weeks, but because I don't know how to plan, I do it the night before it is due. Go to page 115 for help.

36. I have so many ideas floating around in my head, I have trouble organizing my writing. Go to page 117 for help.

37. I don't know how to write a paragraph. Go to page 119 for help.

38. Assignments pile up on me and I get really stressed. I end up having a "hissy fit." Go to page 122 for help.

39. I don't remember the information I have read in my textbooks. Go to page 125 for help.

40. I have trouble remembering the vocabulary words. Go to page 127 for help.

41. I have tried everything you suggested, and I still have homework problems. Go to page 131 for help.

Appendix Turn to page 133
Begin Today to Plan for a Brighter Future Turn to page 135
P.M. Daily Activity Log Turn to page 139
Model Planning Steps Turn to page 142
Book Report Turn to page 144

Please note: Though teachers are both male and female, for ease in reading I have referred to the teacher in the masculine form throughout this book.

The 3rd Step:

Read the possible solutions to each challenge and make a promise to try the strategies.

The 4th Step:

Be aware: Changing poor habits takes effort and is not easy.
If you are willing to stick with the strategy, you will enjoy
the results.

The 5th Step:

Set a goal. Make it simple. Write your goal here:

_____

_____

_____

Did you give up
the first time you fell
off your bike?

Every suggestion in this book is like learning to ride a bike, scooter or surfboard. It wasn't easy at first, but you kept trying. You got better every time you tried, until you didn't have to think about it and you could ride with ease.

If you regularly practice the strategies in this book, you will find they can become a part of you.

Important Notice:

If you have problems managing paper and keeping track of materials, you are not dumb. Someday you may have an assistant to take care of this stuff. For now, it will make your life easier and your school life more pleasant if you practice using these strategies.

Consider these strategies the medicine for your problem. I wear eyeglasses to help me see. Someone with homework sickness can use the day planner system as his or her medicine.

Making one change in your homework pattern
will make a huge difference in how well you do.

You don't need to change everything at once. If you make a commitment to make one change a month, you will be amazed at the success you will experience.

I don't like doing it because it is boring.

I understand exactly how you feel. Homework is definitely less exciting than watching T.V. or playing video games. However, think about how completing your homework can make you feel, compared to not doing the work and having to face a poor grade or other negative consequences. Which is more painful?

First, I would like you to describe in words or pictures how you feel when you go to class without the work completed:

#1 _____

_____

_____

Now I would like you to describe how you feel when you have completed all the work and turned it in on time. You can use words or draw a picture.

#2 _____

_____

_____

There are times in our lives when we have to do tasks we just don't want to do. If you can convince yourself that the activity, though boring, is less painful when it is done than when it is not done, then you might find the job a little easier.

If you focus on "it is boring," your mind is getting the wrong message. Try saying to yourself, "I will feel much better when this is done. I need to get this over with now."

"Do it now!" can become your motto. Try it; it may be just the thing to help you get the work done. I had a student who decided all he needed to do was put a sign above his desk that read "DO IT NOW." Once he put up the sign, he never forgot his homework again.

We often avoid doing those things we do not like. The problem is that the task is always in the back of our minds, taking away a little bit of the fun we try replacing it with. Which feeling would you like to repeat, feeling #1 or feeling #2?

You have control over how you feel. Sometimes the feeling of pain while doing the boring assignment is better than the feeling of failure you might have when you arrive to class without completing assignments.

Learning to use positive self-talk, convincing yourself that it isn't so bad to have to complete this work, will help. When you are older and get a job, your boss will expect you to do work that is not always interesting. There will be times when you have to convince yourself that your paycheck is worth putting up with the boring stuff. You may not be getting paid to do homework, but this lesson will help you deal with job challenges later.

You can use the following words to help change your attitude about boring homework:

"I like the feeling of turning in work and knowing that I am demonstrating how smart I am."

"I know that this assignment is not fun or exciting, but I would rather get it over with and do something fun when I am finished."

"I need to do this now! I may not like it, but I need to do it now."

"If I do this work now, it won't be hanging in the back of my mind."

"I can do this. I just have to put my mind to it."

When you sit down to do your homework, do the job that is the most challenging first. Attack the part that is boring and get it out of the way. Avoiding it will cause you to spend too much time completing your work. Attack it and be done with it!

In the adult world, no one who hires you is going to care if the work is boring. They won't be impressed with "I have an IQ of 156, and I don't see the need to do this work." Learning how to complete work that is uninteresting and boring is training for life.

Did you know you don't have to be great at every subject? Often students think a subject or assignment is boring because it is easier to say "I'm bored" than to say "I'm not good at this." As you improve your skills you will find your attitude will change.

I lose papers.

Many people have a hard time with organizing papers. They do not know how to keep everything neat and tidy. I have always had a problem knowing what to do with a pile of papers.

If you have a problem with paper management, you need a system to keep the papers organized. Chances are no one has ever told you why a notebook is important. It is a place where you can put a paper and the paper will be there when you need it. If you throw your papers in a book bag or shove them in your desk, you will not be sure where to find them and you will waste time looking for them.

Step 1: Get yourself a three-ring binder, preferably one with pockets on the inside covers. You will also need folders for each subject that will fit inside the binder. Include a pencil holder in your notebook that can be clipped onto the rings. Use it for a highlighting pen, a few pencils, colored pencils, an eraser that does not leave smudges, and ink pens—one red, one green and several blue and black. It is also helpful to have a manual pencil sharpener and a three-hole punch. Be sure to have the paper you need for each subject: notebook paper, computer paper, graph paper, etc.

Step 2: Since organizing material is not easy for you, it requires effort. You will have to concentrate every time you receive a paper. Taking a paper and shoving it in your bag or desk should no longer be acceptable. You have to say to yourself, **"I must take this paper and put it in its proper place. I need to do it now!"** Self-talk is a helpful method. It's almost like having a mom in your head. Try being firm with yourself. **It will never be easy,** because your brain does not work that way, but it will gradually become a pattern. For this reason, you must concentrate on what you are doing. Soon you will find yourself doing it without thinking.

There may be times when you fall into your old pattern. When you get too confident and feel it is no longer important to put papers in the day planner, you will begin to lose papers again. If this happens, all you have to do is remind yourself that this is not easy for you and say to yourself, "I must always put my papers in their proper place." Do not be too hard on yourself! Realize that correcting a bad habit takes time. Sometimes we take two steps forward and one step backward. The main thing is that you keep moving forward toward better habits.

Step 3: What is its proper place? If you are using more than one folder, label your folders with the subject names. Do not allow yourself to put the language paper in the math folder. When I follow this system, I can find papers easily and I waste less time. When I slip back into my old pattern, I spend more time looking for the work than it takes to do the work.

If you have a problem with using too many folders, you might consider using the pockets of your three-ring binder instead. Use the front pocket of the day planner for work that needs to be completed and the pocket at the back for work that is completed. Your goal every evening, before you go to bed, should be to have the front pocket of your day planner emptied and the back pocket full of the work that will be turned in the next day. If the system is simple, it will be easier to follow.

Step 4: Use a day planner. It will help you keep track of your assignments. It should fit in your notebook. It is a place to list all activities that need to be completed. Developing the habit of recording all assignments and commitments and looking at the planner on a daily basis will ensure your success. Breaking up projects and long-term assignments into small tasks and recording them in the planner will allow you to tackle large projects and not become overwhelmed. It is always best to schedule the most difficult tasks to be completed first, leaving the simplest tasks for last. Are you the type of student who wants to take the full two weeks to complete a project or do you prefer getting it done in three days? Whichever you prefer, **plan for it.**

I forget the materials I need to complete the assignment.

Chances are you are not naturally organized. This is why you forget materials. There is a solution. Try asking yourself every day, "Do I have what I need to complete the assignment?" If you do not, you must collect the materials before you leave the classroom. Stop before you leave the class, open your day planner, carefully look at each item on your homework list, ask yourself if you have what is needed, check to see if it is in your day planner or book bag and place everything in your book bag.

"The teacher didn't give it to me" is a frequent comment made by some students. This is not a good excuse. Realize that you are responsible for what you need. Do not wait for someone to give it to you. Ask the teacher. The teacher may be so busy that he will not always be able to keep track of every student. It is best if you put yourself in charge of you, and you won't be disappointed because you will have what you need to be successful.

Place the materials you will need in your three-ring binder. See the answer to #2 for information on what you need to help organize your materials. Keeping a binder for homework will provide a place to put the materials you will need. They will be where you need them when you sit down to do your homework.

Never leave school without the materials you will need to be successful. Ask yourself, **"Do I have what I need to be successful tonight?"** Then double-check your homework notebook to be sure you have everything.

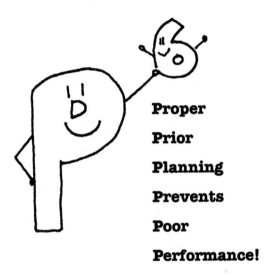

Proper

Prior

Planning

Prevents

Poor

Performance!

I am not performing as well as I think I should.

If you have been putting adequate time into studying and you are not waiting until the last minute to prepare for tests, it can be very disappointing if you do not perform well. If you are studying a little every evening, you will have more success than if you wait to study the night before a test.

Are you a marathon studier? Do you cram all your studying into the last six hours the night before the test? We remember those items we look at first when studying and the items we see at the end of a study period. We call these first and last experiences. Try breaking your study time into fifteen-minute periods. It will give you more first and last learning experiences. These experiences will get the information into your long-term memory and you will likely remember more of what you study.

Are you studying material the proper way for your learning style? Everyone learns differently. One person may need to see something to remember it. Someone else may need to build an object. Another student may need to talk about the subject matter, while still another student may need to act out the concept. There are other students who may need to study in several ways to remember information. Try different methods of studying to determine which works best for you.

If you learn best by hearing information:

- Study with someone who will discuss the concepts with you.

- Talk through your assignments.

- Memorize rules by saying them aloud.

- Sub-vocalize while you read quietly.

- Record the chapters and listen to the tapes.

If you learn best by seeing information:

- Create charts using different colors. Your mind will create a mental picture and you will be able to close your eyes and see the chart in your mind's eye.

- Color code concepts.

- Create note cards for studying.

- Take notes during class. You will be able to see what is being said.

- Create pictures of math facts and memorize the pictures.

If you need to be active during learning:

- Create a song about the information and dance to it.

- Use objects to help you work out problems.

- Walk on a treadmill or ride a stationary bike while you read.

- Divide study periods into fifteen-minute segments and do something active in between.

Are you learning from mistakes? Reviewing your work will assure you that the teacher is giving you the credit you deserve.

Did you know that the answers in the Teacher's Manual could be incorrect? If you miss an answer on a worksheet, go over your work to see what you missed and why. Ask the teacher why you missed the question.

Explain that you want to see where your thinking was incorrect. Do you look in the book for the reason you gave an answer and then show the teacher why you answered the way you did? "Mr. ____, in the book it says... and that is why I answered the question the way I did. Can you show me how my thinking was off?" Show your teacher proof for your answers.

Are you talking to your teacher and asking questions to find out how you can improve in the class?

The following are words you can learn to help improve your performance in class. Students who speak to their teachers in the following ways demonstrate that they are interested in doing well. The teacher will be impressed that you care enough to ask.

"Mr. ____, I am not doing well and I don't know why. Can you tell me what I am doing wrong?"

"Mr. ____, I studied for the test for several days and I still did not do very well. Can you give me some ideas that will help me do better on the next test?"

"Mr. ____, can you suggest the best way to study for this class?"

"Mr. ____, I am not good at planning. Can you suggest the best order in which to do this project?"

"Mr. ____, this is the answer I got for #3. Can you show me where I went wrong?"

"Mr. ____, I tried several different ways to do #26. Can you show me another way, so I can understand it?"

"Mr. ____, I thought I understood the concept you taught yesterday, but when I got home I went blank. Can you show me another way to help me understand?"

"Mr. ____, I really want to do well in this class. Can you tell me what I can do to improve?"

"Mr. ____, may I turn in my research project early so you can tell me if I am on the right track and doing it correctly?"

"Mr. ____, when can I meet with you to go over the concepts so I am sure I understand them?"

"Mr. ____, could you illustrate or draw a picture of the concept on the board? I am a visual learner and am having trouble understanding what you are saying."

There is a chance the teacher will not care about your desire to improve. Do not let that stop you from asking someone else who cares. Don't let one person stop you from being the best student you can be. I always tell my students to think about the worst thing that could happen if they ask a question - the teacher won't help them and they will be in the same place.

What is the best thing that could happen if you ask? You could get help.

Very few teachers will be rude. Most of the time, when you ask a question, there are twenty other students who have the same question. **You will be the one who gets help, if you ask.**

Are you absolutely sure you understand what the teacher wants you to do? You can ask the teacher, "I want to be sure I'm doing the correct assignment. Am I supposed to _____?" The teacher can clarify the directions and this will improve your performance.

I do the work, but I forget it at home.

BOY! MY PACK IS LIGHT TODAY.

YOU FORGOT ME!

HOME WORK

Chances are you do not manage papers well. It is not your fault. Some things you just have to be taught. You can learn how to manage papers, but you must have a system and take care of the papers whenever you have finished an assignment. You need to make an effort and be deliberate about tending to the papers. You can say to yourself, **"I must put this paper in its proper place."** It is important to follow all the following homework steps:

1. Record your assignment in your day planner.

2. Place the paper to be completed in the front pocket of the notebook.

3. Complete the work at home.

4. Place the work in the back pocket of the notebook.

5. Highlight the assignment in your day planner. This indicates that the work is completed and in the correct place. It also makes it very apparent when there are assignments that require your attention.

6. Place your notebook in your backpack.

7. Place the backpack near the door from which you will leave.

Checking your day planner every evening at 7:00 p.m. is an excellent habit to develop. In this way you will be sure everything is completed.

I cannot tell you how many times I have organized my materials and walked right out the door without them. I have to put my things in a spot that requires me to pick them up in order to open the door. It will take concentration to do this, but after a while you will find it is a successful method for remembering your work.

You Can Do This!
It may be challenging, but you can do this!

I don't know where to begin, so I avoid doing the work.

Many students have difficulty knowing how to get started. Using a day planner is helpful. It requires you to record each assignment as it is given. Label the most difficult assignment or the one that is due first with an **"A."** Label the next most difficult assignment **"B."** Continue labeling them.

Begin with the **"A."** assignment and list every step it requires. Do one step at a time. You can only focus on one thing at a time. Once you have completed all the steps, you can place the first assignment in your day planner, highlight the item in your day planner and move on to assignment **"B."**

It's easier to eat an elephant one bite at a time.

Often we let a problem stop us. If the first question is one you do not understand, skip it and go on to the next question. Many times the answer to one question is in the wording of another question. Once you find a question you can do, you will feel more confident. Your teacher will be impressed if you explain that you did not understand one question, but attempted the others.

Don't give up!

I don't always understand the questions or the directions.

Learning to understand directions and questions is easy if you learn the cue words.

If the question starts with the word **"who,"** the answer will be a person's name.

If the question starts with the word **"what,"** the answer will be a thing.

If the question starts with the word **"where,"** the answer will be a place.

If the question begins with the word **"why,"** the answer will be a reason.

Learning to understand questions also requires you to focus on key words. Sometimes you will come across a word in a question that you do not understand. It is important to know the meaning of all the words in the question before you try to answer the question. Once you understand all the words, the question will become clearer.

It is helpful to highlight the key words of the question so you can focus on the main idea. You eliminate the extra words and it helps make the question clear.

Sample Question: List the words that are synonyms for "happy."

To answer this question, you would highlight the words **list** and **synonyms**. They are the important words that will lead to understanding the question. **List tells you what is expected of you** - the "to do" word. **Synonym is the word you would look up.** Once you looked it up, you would learn that synonyms are "words that mean the same." **The definition is the key that unlocks the meaning of the question.**

Pay attention to cue words such as number words. When the direction is "List two spelling words that have the same pattern," you will need to write two words. If the direction is **"Describe two ways** a river is formed," you will need to use words in sentences to describe **two ways**.

Use the process of elimination when trying to do fill-in type questions. For example, if you are given the definitions of words and you are to identify the word that matches the definition, you can go through the list and look for all the words that could fit the definition. Once you have eliminated all the words that do not fit, you can look up the remaining words in the dictionary. Again, the dictionary can be like a key that unlocks the meaning of the question. You should have a dictionary and a thesaurus at your study area.

It is very important to read all the questions and directions before you leave class to see if there is anything the teacher can clarify. The teacher can provide strategies to help you understand the question if he knows this is a difficult task for you. You will help him do a better job if you let him know what you need to learn. If you have your mom or dad help you, the teacher never knows what you didn't know how to do. He will assume that you know how to do this type of work and he will continue to give you more of the same work. Don't wait until you get home to look at the assignment; then it is too late to get effective help.

Help your teacher do the best job he can by asking him to show you ways to improve your skills at reading questions.

I never seem
to have enough
time to get
everything
done.

If time management is not your strength, you can do many things to help yourself. First you need some time-management tools. They are a monthly planner, weekly planner, daily planner and stopwatch or minute timer.

Often students get into trouble because they do not have an accurate understanding of time. Time can just slip away, especially if they get interested in an activity. Before they know it, hours have gone by and it is time to go to bed. Try using some of the following strategies to help yourself. (You will find samples of planning sheets in the Appendix.)

Being aware of exactly how much time you have is the first step.

- Using the monthly calendar, record any future projects.

- Using the weekly calendar, record all school and non-school activities, athletic events, meetings, doctor's visits, etc.

- Using the daily schedule, record the day's schedule. Be sure to block out travel time to and from your activities. Block out time to eat, have fun, dress, bathe and brush your teeth.

You may notice that you have only a few half-hour opportunities to get work done. You may find that you need to do some work in the car as you travel from place to place. You may even decide to get started on your work during lunch or recess. You may also need to get up early to complete work that you can't complete in the evening. (I am leery of this strategy because you don't always have adequate time to complete the work before leaving for school. You are setting yourself up for failure if you wait to do the work in the morning.)

Proper Prior Planning Prevents Poor Performance.

Knowing how many activities you have after school will help you use your time wisely.

Those who are busy get the most done.

They know they don't have any extra time, so they need to plan carefully.

If you are burdened with too many assignments because your teachers do not consult one another, don't be afraid to approach a teacher and let him know. Teachers forget that you have more than one class.

You can say the following to the teacher:

"Mr. ____, I was wondering if we could reschedule our test for Monday instead of Tuesday, since we have three tests on Tuesday." Asking to have the test earlier than scheduled indicates you are planning ahead.

I don't know how
to do some of
the tasks
I have to
do to complete
the assignment.

Many times, teachers think a student has knowledge that he or she does not have. If a student goes home and asks a parent for help, the teacher never knows he didn't have the skills needed to complete the assignment.

The best thing you can do is to tell the teacher that you do not know how to do the activity. Tell your teacher that you have never been taught how to outline, research, plan a project or organize a group project. You may need to be taught how to break projects into bite-sized pieces.

You can say, **"I want to do the best job I can, but I do not know how to outline. Can you tell me a time when I can come in and get some help?"**

If you do not understand a concept the teacher has just taught, be sure to get help. You can ask the teacher to show you a different way of doing the problem, since you didn't understand the first way you were shown. If you are a visual learner, you may need to ask the teacher to illustrate the concept for you. If you are a kinesthetic learner, you will need to ask the teacher to show you or demonstrate the concept to you. If you are an auditory learner, you will need to hear the explanation or read the directions aloud.

I seem to get distracted easily while I am doing my homework.

Students without an established time limit can get easily distracted. If you use the daily time scheduler described in #8, you learn how little time you have to do homework. If you know you have only a half-hour to complete an assignment, you will find you pay closer attention.

If you have hours of free time, you may want to give yourself an artificial time restraint. Tell yourself that you need to complete this assignment by 7:00 p.m. Act as if you have something else to do. This will help you stay on track. You will be much more productive. If you think you have all the time in the world, you will end up wasting it.

Some students use a minute timer. They set the timer for five minutes and mark where they are in their home-work. They see how much they can accomplish in five minutes. As your concentration improves, you can increase the time.

If you are distracted by ideas that pop into your head, you may find keeping a journal very helpful. Recording the idea saves it so you can come back to it when you have time to explore it at greater length. "Sticky notes" are also helpful to keep you on track. By recording your distracting idea, you can get it out of your mind and you will be able to focus.

Sometimes playing soft music can help you stay focused. Try studying for short periods. Study for fifteen minutes and then get up and move around. It will help you get the most out of your homework time.

My daughter has to walk on a treadmill or ride a stationary bike to concentrate. She is very kinesthetic and she can concentrate much better when her larger muscles are in use.

If your schedule allows, treat yourself to something fun if you complete your work in a timely fashion.

You may need to apply some self-talk. This is a technique that requires you to talk to yourself. The following are some statements you can say to yourself to help you stay on task:

"I need to focus on what I need to do."

"I need to wait to play until all my work is done."

"I will feel better once this work is completed and out of the way."

To help you stay on task, you might make a very specific list of each task you need to complete for each assignment. It is not clear enough to say, "I have work to do on my report." You must be very specific as to each item to be done. The following list gives examples of specific directions:

1. Check out books on your topic.

2. Take notes on note cards from each source. Record the number of the book you are using. #1 book is *The Encyclopedia Britannica*, Vol. 6, page 122. Each note card should have a topic heading so the notes from several sources can be placed on the appropriate card. For example, if you were doing a report on an animal, you would need one note card for each of the following topics: habitat, food or prey, appearance, behavior. Any information from source #1 would have a #1 in front of it. When you are finished taking notes, all the information on habitat will be in one place.

3. Decide on the order of the report. Which topic do you want to be first? Then write a paragraph or two for each topic card.

4. Do a rough draft of your report.

5. Have a friend or family member edit it for you, checking for misspellings and punctuation errors. You can even ask your teacher to read it and make suggestions on ways it can be improved, provided you do so prior to the due date.

6. Write a final draft.

If your teacher has requested other items, you can add them to the list. Do one thing at a time. As you do, highlight the completed task. Breaking the assignment into parts will help you stay focused. You won't become as overwhelmed if you can do little steps, one at a time.

When I ask for help, the adults say, "You're smart, go figure it out."

Teachers and parents get very frustrated when students say, "I don't get it." They perceive it as a lazy way out. Using different words might avoid this type of reaction from them.

Oftentimes, parents don't understand that you do not know where to begin when trying to answer a question. Try to identify what you do not understand. Is it a word that needs defining? Is it a process that is unclear? Then try changing the way you ask for help. Instead of saying "I don't get it," say "I don't know what is meant by 'synonym' in question seven."

The best way to understand a question is to start with the question words. Is it a Who, What, Where, Why or When question?

Read the suggestions for #7. They will give you some tips that will help you figure out the question.

I don't seem
to understand
the concepts
I study.

It is important to be sure that you understand concepts that you study. The best way to be sure you are grasping concepts is to ask the teacher to check your thinking. Explain the concept to the teacher and see if you are on the right track.

Pay attention to headings, captions, bold words and the questions at the end of the book. These will give you ideas on what to focus on as you read. You will remember more of what you have read if you review the questions at the end of the chapter before you begin to read.

Vocabulary, or the language of the subject, is the most important key to understanding what you are studying. Record all the words you do not understand and look them up in the dictionary or glossary. Then go back and reread the information. You will find you understand more of what you read.

Stop after each sentence and summarize to yourself. We often read without paying attention. In a sense, we are just reading words and not understanding the meaning. Read and summarize often to force yourself to concentrate.

Use "sticky notes" to record key information. If you need to search for answers after the reading, you will not have to reread every word.

The teacher
returns my
graded work
and says
I can do better,
but I don't
know how.

Teachers look for many things when grading papers. The following are ways to check the quality of your paper:

- Is your work done neatly? You need to "dress your paper for success." It should have a heading. The margins should be about one inch on each side. Your work should be legible. Be sure to use your best handwriting.

- Reread the question and highlight the key words. Did you answer the question?

- Did you do the assignment? If you were to do the even-numbered items, did you instead do the odd-numbered items?

- Look at specific words in the question. Sometimes one word can make a difference in what is expected of you. Pay attention to key words.

- Don't be discouraged. Ask the teacher what you can do to improve your work. Ask him to be specific. You can say, "Mr. ___, I would like to improve this paper; could you show me how I can improve it?"

- Try completing the assignment a few days prior to its due date. Ask the teacher for his opinion and you will get valuable feedback as to whether you are on the right track. See #15 for more ideas.

- Each teacher looks for different qualities in your work. Learn to ask for more specifics from your teachers. You can ask, "What will you be specifically looking for in this assignment?"

I think I've written an excellent essay, but I get a lower grade than I expected.

Every teacher looks for different elements in essays. Many teachers will give you very clear directions for essays. Some, on the other hand, are not as clear.

Students are not aware that they can ask a teacher to read an essay well before it is due to see if they are going in the right direction. Try asking your teacher the following question: "Mr. ____, could I get you to read my essay to see if I am on the right track? Could you give me some suggestions as to how I can improve my essay?" Your teacher will be impressed with your preparedness. By completing your essay prior to the due date, you are demonstrating that you are a serious student. By asking the teacher to give his input, you are actually getting a second chance to give the teacher what he wants.

Many students find out what the teacher thinks of their essay when they receive the graded essay. Getting feedback from a teacher before the essay is due is a wonderful way to improve your chances of better performance. Asking a peer to read your essay might also be helpful.

Be sure to "dress your paper for success." Believe it or not, a neat and tidy paper can receive a better grade than the same paper that is messy. Be sure to use your best cursive writing when doing written work. Precise margins will give your paper an organized look. Using the proper spacing can give the impression that the paper was written with care. Proofreading your paper can make a world of difference. Your ideas may be well stated, but careless errors will create a negative impression.

I hate the work, so I rush through it and get a poor grade.

Nothing is more irritating to a teacher than receiving work that is less than the student's best. You may not want to do the work, but we all have to do things we don't like. Your work is a reflection of you. If you turn in work that is of poor quality, you are saying that you don't care what others think about you. You are sending the message that you are careless and incapable of doing a good job. You know better than that, but your teacher doesn't. It may be irritating for a few moments to turn out better-quality work, but in the end your scores will improve if you simply slow down and give your work the care it deserves. If you feel it doesn't deserve your care, then you might try a change of attitude. **Simply telling yourself that you enjoy turning in a quality product will improve your performance.**

I think I understand the homework, but when I get home I can't remember what to do.

Many times we think we understand something until we have to sit down and do it. There are several strategies you can use:

- You can read the questions again, and see if you can find the key words to help unlock the question.

- You can close your eyes and try to visualize the teacher explaining it. Transport yourself back to the classroom. Sometimes reviewing the class session will trigger an idea that will help you figure out what to do.

- Call a classmate and ask him to review with you.

- Try a different way of doing the problem and if you still are not successful, go to school early and ask to speak with your teacher. **Say the following to the teacher:** "I thought I understood what I was supposed to do, but when I got home I discovered I really didn't understand the homework. Could you explain the work to me again?" Coming to class early demonstrates your desire to do well.

- There is a chance that the teacher will not be happy that you did not understand the work. Don't let that discourage you. Try to find a student who understands the concepts to review with you or a teacher from another class. Some teachers don't make as much sense as others. Explain to the other teacher that you asked your teacher for help and for some reason, you still don't understand. Ask if this teacher could try to explain the concept to you. Some teachers will take the time and others will not. Be prepared that you might not get what you want, but you will never know unless you ask.

- Be sure to look at your next assignment carefully. Try doing a problem before you leave class. **Ask the teacher,** "Will you check my work to be sure I am doing it correctly?"

I asked my parents to help me get the materials I need. Now they won't let me do the work

I LOVE PROJECTS!

HERE! LET ME WRITE IT FOR YOU.

myself.

You need to be assured that your parents love you. They want you to succeed. It's not that they don't think you can do the job alone, they just want to help you create the best project possible. They don't realize that your best is good enough for the teacher.

The problem is that teachers don't want your parent's work; they want your work. You can handle this very easily. You can say, **"Mom, I know you want to help me, but I can do this work myself. I really want to do this work by myself. I want to be proud of my work and if you do anything on my project, it's no longer my work."**

I have to do
a group project
and my
partners
never do
their fair share.

Doing a group project is always a challenge. Remember that not all students know how to organize their time or materials. Knowing who can manage them and who can't will help you to avoid last minute problems.

Have a meeting with your group. The following are actions you can take at the meeting to avoid misunderstandings:

1. Make a list of all the jobs that must be completed. Decide who is going to do each job. One person will need to be the leader. This person will be responsible for coordinating all the material. This person needs to be organized and responsible.

2. Create a calendar. Decide when each job should be completed. If possible, select dates seven to ten days before the actual due date.

3. The leader should check the progress of each group member. Frequent checks by the leader are necessary. Do not assume that everyone will do the assigned job. It is better to find out that a member has not done his or her job a week before it is due, rather than the day before it is due.

4. There will always be people who will get your grade without earning it. They are not getting a true gift. The student who does the work learns what is important. If you put more value on the grade, then you are missing the value of the activity. The goal of the activity is learning how to get along in a group.

Learning to manage the non-producers in your group takes a lot of skill. Don't let them get by without doing their fair share. You have a right to tell them that you do not think it is fair that you have to do their part. Allowing for enough reminder time may make a difference, but you do have to be prepared that it might not.

Too many times I hear students say, "It isn't fair that I have to do this project with 'flakes.'" The reality is that every group has non-productive members. It is better to learn how to get along with them. You will never be able to avoid them completely.

I have a hard
time turning in
work that is
not perfect.

You have been conditioned to think that it is possible to do everything perfectly. You will drive yourself crazy. No one can do everything perfectly.

Consider why you feel this is even a reasonable or realistic expectation. Are you afraid of making a mistake? Do you think others will think you are dumb? The truth is everyone makes mistakes.

Mistakes are inevitable. Many mistakes have led scientists to wonderful discoveries. The "sticky note" was a huge mistake. If the scientist had been concerned with his work being perfect, he would never have discovered the new glue.

Mistakes are also a wonderful tool. If you look at mistakes as something wonderful that you can learn from, you won't be so concerned about perfection.

Is someone in your family telling you that your work has to be perfect? If so, you might want to share with them that your teacher learns a great deal from your mistakes. It tells him what you need to learn. It is a valuable part of learning. If you are afraid to make mistakes, you won't learn as much as you are capable of learning. Of course, you don't want to use the fact that you can make mistakes as an excuse to do less than your best. But your best should be good enough for any teacher.

Let yourself off the hook! Once you allow yourself to make mistakes you will feel less stress. Trade "Oh no! I made a mistake." for "Wow, what can I learn from this mistake? How can I grow from this mistake?"

Truly successful people are not afraid to make mistakes. They are what we call risk takers. They realize that sometimes to get ahead you have to make mistakes. Babe Ruth struck out 3,582 times. Thomas Edison failed 1,000 times to find the filament that made the light bulb work. It was his 1,001st try that worked.

Try laughing at a mistake you make. It is a good feeling to be relieved of the pressure to be perfect. Practice saying, "I made a mistake. I learn a lot from my mistakes." When you make a mistake, you won't be so hard on yourself.

I can't concentrate at home.

Try several approaches to find the one that works for you. Find a place to work where it is quiet. Ask your family members to have quiet time while you do your work.

You may need to find your own thinking room. Some children find the bathroom a good place to get ideas. Because it is a small room, it has very few distractions.

If you have been in class all day, you may need a break. You may need some physical activity to get the blood flowing to your brain. Play a game of tennis, go for a walk or run around the block before beginning your homework. You might even need to plan some library time where the environment encourages concentration.

Playing soft music while you study can help drown out distractive noise.

Earplugs can also be helpful. Blocking out all noise might be what works best for you.

Everyone else in
my class can do
the work quickly,
which makes
me feel
really dumb.

It is common for you to compare yourself to other students. It is not fair to you to judge yourself by the work of others. Try looking at who you are as a learner. You may be very creative or artistic, while others might be better at math. Instead of focusing on what you don't do well, focus on your abilities. You would be surprised at how many students feel the same way you do. They are probably thinking that you are better than they are at some things.

Try focusing on how much you are improving. Look at your work each day and make a mental note about what you can do today that you could not do one month ago. Try to find one thing each day that you did well. Before you know it, you will be doing better. Your attitude has so much to do with how well you do in school. You don't have to be the brightest child in school if you have a good attitude and never give up!

Every student learns differently. Some children need to hear what they are reading, while others need to form a mental picture to help them understand what they are reading. Other children need "think time" before they can create or write. Quick workers don't always produce clever work. They get the work done quickly, but it is plain. Those students who don't get started right away and who think awhile may come up with more creative and interesting work. You may be one who likes to contemplate or think deeply about questions asked.

Each of our brains works differently. If you are a deep thinker, you may have your opportunity to think stolen by a person who blurts out answers. Once someone blurts out an answer, it stops the thought process. You have the right as a learner to ask those who blurt out answers to write down their idea so you have ample time to think. You also have the right to ask your teacher if he can have the class write down ideas so you have time to think. You could say, "Mr. ____, I need time to think and it is hard for me to get my ideas organized when people blurt out. Could we have some quiet 'think time' so I can think about your questions?"

If your teacher isn't interested in your idea, you can do your best. Just don't be too hard on yourself if you are not given enough "think time." It isn't your fault and it certainly does not mean you are dumb.

Be kind to yourself.

I don't have a place to study at home. It's too noisy.

If you need a place to study, discuss this with your parents. If the kitchen table is the only place to do your homework, ask if the family could have quiet hour when no TV or radio is used. It could also become a quiet reading time for your parents.

If this is not possible, consider staying at school and beginning your homework immediately after school. You could also ask your parents to drop you off at the public library, where you can find large tables and a quiet environment.

You can ask your parent to purchase some waxed earplugs for you. I had a very noisy environment at home and no cooperation from my siblings. The earplugs helped me make it all the way through college. I actually use them now when I am trying to complete thoughts as I write my books. A simple sound can sometimes steal an idea away from me, so I use the earplugs when I need to concentrate.

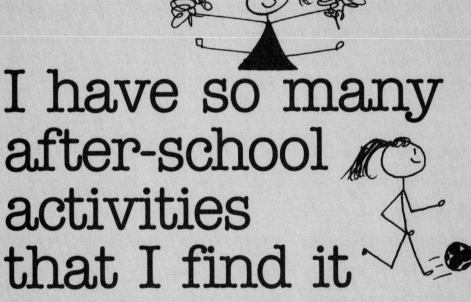

I have so many
after-school
activities
that I find it
hard to start
my homework
before 8:00 p.m.

This is a difficult problem in today's society. Parents want to offer their children varied opportunities to explore different interests. This does present a challenge to students. More than ever, students need to keep a day planner. You will need to be aware of activities you have planned along with the assignments that are due. Your first priority should be your schoolwork. If you are overburdened, it may be necessary to ask your parent to postpone a tap class or a soccer practice. If you plan properly, you will be able to enjoy all your activities and still do well in school. The key is in "Proper Prior Planning."

It is said that busy people get the most done. This is true, because busy people know they cannot leave anything to the last minute. They plan well ahead and get projects completed before due dates. At the end of this book are some schedules. If followed, they will help you juggle all that you have to do.

It is very important to consider your schedule before you commit to any outside activities. A soccer coach is going to expect you to show up to practices and games. If you miss too many practices, you are letting down the coach and your teammates. It is better to pass on the sport than to do it half way.

Using daily and monthly schedulers and sticking to them will help you balance your life.

I'm a procrastinator.

It is human nature to procrastinate. However, procrastination creates a tremendous amount of stress. Just thinking about what you have to do can occupy your mind and cause you to expend unnecessary mental energy. If you use the schedulers at the back of this book, you will find that you are less likely to procrastinate.

Procrastination is one of the biggest reasons students don't do the best job possible. The work is left to the last minute, not allowing for adequate proofing or creative thinking. Your work, when rushed, is not always your best effort. You may even run out of time and find yourself with an incomplete project. Procrastination causes headaches and stomach aches. It puts undue stress on your body and will have a negative impact on your performance.

Students who study at the last minute do not do as well in the long run as students who study several days before a test. When you cram the night before a test, you are putting your body in a stressed state. You go to the test tired and unsure of yourself. The lack of self-confidence gets in the way of doing well. Your mind shuts down when it is under stress, so all the information you tried to cram into your brain the night before gets closed off. If you study for five days prior to a test and give your subject a little time each evening, you are allowing the information to make it into your long-term memory and you are more likely to remember it. All you will have to do is close your eyes, relax and the information will come to you.

The easy solution for procrastination is to create a plan and make a commitment to stick to it. See the schedulers at the end of this book and try using them for one month. You will be amazed at how much easier they will make your life. You will feel self assured and calm.

I'm told to study, but I don't know how!

Many students are not aware of the variety of ways to prepare for a test. Students need to try different methods of study to learn which one works best for them. The following are methods you can try until you find the one that works best for you:

- Make note cards of bold-faced words or formulas to help you study for a test. Writing the note card is the first step in studying, so don't be tempted to use someone else's note cards. Write the vocabulary word on one side of the card and the definition on the other side. Vocabulary is the key to unlocking the meaning of many questions, so mastering the vocabulary is a very important part of successful test taking.

- Create a diagram illustrating the main ideas of the material you are studying.

- Use different colors to help you see patterns. Seeing the patterns in subjects will help you retain information.

- When learning spelling words, try writing each letter of a word with a different color to help you see each letter. Look for the words inside words. Write your words on graph paper and outline each one so you can see the shape of the word. Write the word several times and be sure you spell it correctly when practicing. Look at the word to become familiar with its appearance. Determine anything about the word that might give you a problem (an irregular spelling or a silent letter). If you are an auditory learner, write the word and say it aloud. You can also practice how a word feels in your mouth as you spell it.

• Create a song to help you remember important facts.

• Create a rhyme.

• Use acronyms to help you remember lists of words. An acronym is a word formed from other words. If you were trying to remember the bones of the body you could list the bones in order and using the first letter of each bone, create a nonsense word.

• Create a table of information using abbreviations to help you remember categories of information.

• Using a plastic sheet protector, an erasable pen designed for plastic and a fill-in type worksheet, you can create your own test. You can use the same worksheet over and over by erasing it with a damp cloth.

- Practice writing information on a Dry Erase board.

- Draw illustrations of main ideas. "One picture is worth a thousand words."

- Ask a friend how he or she studied for a test. Many people develop their own methods.

- Study with a friend. Discuss what you learned. Talking about concepts helps to place them in your long-term memory.

- Teach someone else the subject matter. You learn the material differently when you have to explain it to someone else.

You may need to use more than one of these methods when studying. Try many of them until you find the one that works for you. Ask your teacher to recommend some methods that he has found successful.

Never, Never Give Up!

I don't study the correct items for tests.

Many students study everything to prepare for a test. It can be overwhelming to try to learn everything for each test. Try looking at your chapters for the main ideas. These are usually noted by headings or italicized words. The key terms are helpful to learn. Be sure you understand all their meanings. Flash cards are very helpful tools when learning terms. Discussing the topics with your classmates is another helpful study method.

One resource that students rarely use is the teacher. The teacher can tell you what will be on the test if you simply ask, "Mr. ____, is there one part of the material that is more important to pay attention to when I study? I'd like to do well on the test." Or "Mr. ____, what concepts should I focus on when I study? I have difficulty knowing what is important to study and it would be helpful to me to be able to focus on the most important material."

You do have to prepare for the teacher who will not be helpful, but I have found that most teachers are helpful. You will never know unless you ask. The worst thing that can happen is that the teacher won't be of any help. The best thing that can happen is that the teacher will help you focus your studying.

Knowing the type of test that will be given can also be helpful. Ask the teacher, "How will I be tested on this information?" The teacher's answer will help you to decide what pertinent information you should study.

Be sure to thank the teacher for his time. He will appreciate your consideration.

I get easily frustrated and I don't even want to do the work. I just don't care anymore.

When work is difficult for us, it is easy to get frustrated. Your body's first reaction is to protect itself from a negative feeling. Some children go to "LaLa Land" (that great imaginary place where they can instantly be on a beach or out skateboarding) where they can escape horrible feelings. Other children don't like the feeling, but they have learned that if they don't give up, that horrible feeling can turn into a wonderful feeling. Once you overcome something very difficult, you will feel so incredibly wonderful you won't mind other challenges.

Before you can feel successful you need to know what happens to your body when you get frustrated. Your body tenses and no matter how hard you try, you cannot think straight. You may forget the easiest thing if you are tense. I forgot my phone number when someone asked me in a hurry. The person kept saying, "Give it to me now. I said now." For the life of me, I could not remember it.

Our brains are like elevator doors. Have you ever tried opening the doors to an elevator that was full and had to close? It's impossible. You end up having to wait for the next one. Well, when you get frustrated, the elevator doors to your brain slam shut and no matter how hard you try, nothing is going to get in or out. The best way to open the doors to your brain is to relax. Take a deep breath and close your eyes. Visualize the teacher doing the explanation on the board. Picture your teacher giving the directions. Use some of the strategies for other challenges in this book to see if they can help you with the difficult assignment. Sometimes just saying to yourself that you can get this and being willing to try different things to overcome it is all that is necessary to be successful. Here are a few strategies that might assist you:

1. Take a deep breath.

2. Reread the question.

3. Identify words in the question that are unclear.

4. Look up the definitions of unclear words.

5. Skip the question that is giving you difficulty. The answer to one question might be given in the form of another question.

6. Reread the question aloud.

7. Reread the question aloud again. You may need to reread the question seven to ten times before it becomes clear.

8. Realize that no one expects you to be perfect. Ask the teacher for assistance the next day.

My homework takes me three hours.

Are you allowing yourself to be stumped on one problem? Look at #24 for some ideas.

If you are working consistently and your work still takes you three hours, consider informing your teacher of this fact. Teachers assign work assuming it should take a certain amount of time. They do not always know exactly how long it takes a student to do an assignment unless the student reports the time spent. The teacher could be assuming the assignment is taking thirty minutes when it is actually taking one hour and forty-five minutes to complete. Communicate politely to your teacher. "Mr. ____, this assignment took me two hours to complete and I don't know why it is taking me so long."

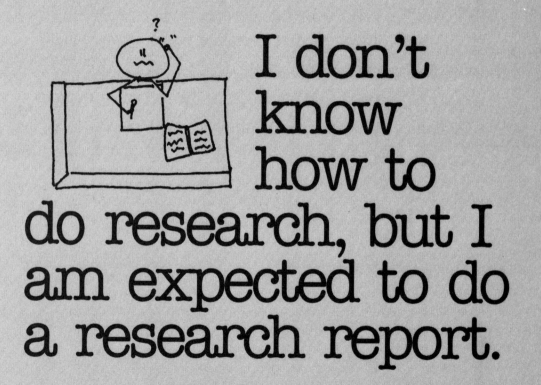

I don't know how to do research, but I am expected to do a research report.

Many times teachers will assign research reports to students who have never been introduced to the process. The teacher assumes that the students have been taught the steps to doing research. Inform the teacher that you have never been taught how to do a report and arrange a time to get special help. By asking for help in this way, you are informing the teacher that you, along with your classmates, have never received this instruction. The teacher many opt to teach the entire class the process, simply because you asked. Your classmates will thank you.

You can try to do a report using the steps that follow:

1. Create a list of questions about what you hope to learn from your research.

2. Turn your questions into headings or topics.

3. Create a note page for each of your headings.

4. Locate books and reference materials you can use to obtain information.

5. Record each reference on a separate page, numbering each book you use. Obtain a bibliography format from your teacher.

6. As you record information on your note pages, record only key words and note the number of the reference and the page number from which the information was obtained.

7. Create a paragraph or two from each topic page.

8. Arrange the paragraphs into a report.

9. Have another student or parent edit your work.

10. Create a final draft of your report.

I don't understand the teacher's directions, but I don't want my classmates to think I am stupid, so I don't ask questions.

You are not alone in your feelings. The most common student fear is of looking stupid in front of his or her peers. The truth is when you have the guts to ask a question, you are actually helping your classmates. I can remember John. He asked thoughtful questions. I thought he was so brave and I had a lot of respect for him. If you have a question, chances are several students in your class have the same question. They are just as afraid to ask as you are and they are equally confused.

I don't see why I should do homework.

Homework can seem like a waste of time. It can be boring and is certainly less exciting than video games and riding a skateboard. It does teach many skills or it teaches us how to deal with unpleasant tasks. It helps in learning how to budget our time and do a job even when we want to do something else.

If we dwell on how much of a waste it is to do homework, time for fun is lost. It is much better to find out what skills you need to complete the work, get help if you need it and do the job as best you can. Then go out and have a good time playing the game of your choice.

Simply make a different decision about how you look at homework and you will be surprised how much easier it is to get it done.

I can't do
my homework
because the
teacher didn't
give me the
worksheet.

WHERE'S
PAGE 2?

pg 1
of 2

A teacher's life is very hectic. There will be times when the teacher forgets to give out a paper he has assigned. Blaming the teacher is not a good excuse. Consider a different approach to your homework. Be in control and be sure that you always have any papers that are assigned, even if you have to ask for them. From today forward, become the student who reminds the teacher to pass out the assignment. If you approach the teacher politely, he will be grateful for the reminder. You will also demonstrate your interest in being a responsible student.

I can't do my homework because I forgot my book or assignment at school.

Arriving home and discovering you left your book at school can produce a horrible feeling and the inability to do the assignment. You have a few options. First, contact a classmate and arrange to borrow his book for the evening. Second, arrive at school early and ask to get your book and do the homework in the library or at the lunch tables. Third, go to the library and check the book out for the evening.

Using a day planner will help you avoid this problem in the future.

Identify how you feel when you discover the book is missing and decide what you will do next time to avoid that feeling.

Some students ask friends to fax a copy of the homework to them. This strategy does not help develop a good homework habit of recording your homework daily and being sure you have the materials before you leave class.

I was supposed
to have a parent
sign my paper,
but she got home
after I went to
bed, so I got
in trouble.

It can be difficult if your parents work late or if they attend meetings and you don't see them. Try problem solving and think of ways to get the paper signed without talking with them. My children would write me a note and put it and the paper on my pillow so I would see it when I went to bed. They would also leave "sticky notes" on my bathroom mirror, on the front door and on the door to the bathroom. Each note stated that they needed the paper on my pillow signed. They would then pick it up in the morning.

If this approach doesn't work, try sharing with the teacher all the things you did to get your parent's attention. The teacher will know you didn't ignore the assignment.

I have a project due in two weeks, but because I don't know how to plan, I do it the night before it is due.

All you need for proper planning is a good calendar and a list of the assignments that are due. Make a list of everything that is required for the project. Decide how much time each activity will take. If you are not sure, ask someone who might.

Schedule the activities on the calendar. The calendar in the Appendix will be helpful. Remember to assign yourself a deadline of at least three days prior to the due date. Record each activity. First do the work you feel will be the hardest and save the easiest activity for last.

Plan for those activities that require a parent to drive you to pick up supplies. Allowing the driver a few days' notice will assure you that you will be able to get someone to help you. Waiting until the last minute will increase the chance that no one will be available.

Decide if you want to complete the work over two weeks or pour your heart into it for three to four days. Whichever you decide, planning for it will avoid being up until the wee hours of the morning the day the project is due.

I have so many ideas floating around in my head, I have trouble organizing my writing.

When it comes time to organize an essay, story or report, it can be frustrating if you have an active mind. Using "sticky notes" to record your ideas is a simple way to organize the ideas that create a distraction to you.

Record each idea on a separate note. Once you have recorded all your ideas, you are free to organize them by moving the pieces around, placing common topics together. Using the wall in your bedroom to arrange the notes is helpful when you have many ideas.

Once you have decided on an order, you are ready to begin the writing. If an idea pops into your head as you are writing, create a new note and place it in the appropriate place.

I don't know how to write a paragraph.

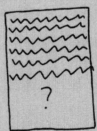

Think of a paragraph as a deli sandwich. To prepare a sandwich, you collect all the ingredients, such as lettuce, tomatoes, meat, cheese, onions, mustard, mayonnaise and the bread. When you write a paragraph, you collect all your ideas. "Sticky notes" provide a wonderful way to organize those ideas. You are able to place one idea or thought on each note. Then decide what order you want them in your paragraph.

Once you decide on the order, you need to deal with the "bun" of your paragraph. The top and bottom of a bun look very much alike, but they are slightly different. The topic sentence and the concluding sentence begin and end your paragraph. They may sound different, but they should have the same meaning. The topic sentence will tell the reader the main idea of the paragraph. The concluding sentence will remind the reader of the main idea of the paragraph.

I like to spice up my paragraphs as someone might spice up a sandwich. My paragraph's mustard and relish are adjectives and descriptive verbs. If you're writing about the way an animal moves, you might look up the word "walk" in a thesaurus and identify its synonyms. As you compose your draft, you will have a whole collection of adjectives and verbs in mind, and your work will have variety and spice.

Assignments pile up on me and I get really stressed. I end up having a "hissy fit."

"Hissy fits" are your body's way of releasing tension. They don't ever solve a challenge. In many cases, a "hissy fit" can be counterproductive. Instead of having the fit, you could have finished the activity.

The best way to avoid "hissy fits" is to plan well for activities. Some teachers have patterns they follow for assigning work. If you can identify this pattern, it will make your life much easier. If a teacher assigns vocabulary every Monday and a math assignment on Tuesdays and you have a Social Studies test on Thursday, you can get a "jump start" on your homework by beginning assignments and studying over the weekend. Begin studying for your Social Studies test by creating note cards, outlining the chapter or summarizing each paragraph of the chapter. Studying for fifteen to twenty minutes each evening is much more beneficial than studying for one or two hours the night before a test. Using the daily schedule in the Appendix will help you identify how much time you actually have to complete assignments. If you know you have only fifteen minutes to complete an assignment, you will be surprised how efficient you can become. If you fail to plan, you will actually be planning to fail. So use the monthly planner to plan projects, the weekly planner to plan for the week and the daily plan sheet to avoid the "hissy fits."

If your teacher is unpredictable, you can take control of your future. Become the student who helps clarify a pattern for the class. Ask questions about when and what type of tests will be given. Demonstrate that you are conscientious and want to plan well. This will help the rest of the class and will allow you to plan for success.

If you like to talk with your friends on the phone, you can schedule "phone time." Phone conversations eat up more time than any other activity. Before you know it, an hour can go by. If a friend phones, you can have your family members ask to have the call returned during your scheduled time. This puts you in control of your own time. Completing your assignments before you talk with your friends will relieve you of stress. You'll see the number of "hissy fits" decrease as you become better at planning.

I don't remember
the information
I have read
in my
textbooks.

Knowing how to read a chapter in a textbook is a skill. Many students open the book and begin reading and when they have come to the last page of the chapter they believe they are finished. There are five basic steps to reading a chapter in any book:

1. Start at the end of the chapter with the questions provided by the authors. There you will find what the authors felt was the most important information or the focus of the chapter. It will guide your reading and help keep you focused on the main ideas.

2. Browse the chapter by looking at the pictures, headings, bold face words and captions.

3. Form questions or curiosities about what you are going to find in the chapter. List these questions on "sticky notes." As you read the chapter, you will be looking for the answers to your questions. This method will help you remember what you have read.

4. As you read the chapter, stop at the end of each paragraph and paraphrase what you have read.

5. Seek the answers to your unanswered questions in other sources.

I have trouble remembering my vocabulary words.

Studying for a vocabulary test can be difficult. First determine if you remember items better if you hear them, see them or write them. You may need to use a combination of these strategies to remember words or facts.

If you are a visual person, you need to see a word frequently to remember it. Forming a mental picture of what the word looks like and a scene that would describe the meaning of the word would be helpful. For example, if the word is "barrage," try visualizing yourself standing in the middle of a basketball court and see many people throwing balls at your head. You were being barraged by basketballs. If I then stated that I was barraged by questions from the students, you would have a clear understanding of the word. To remember the part of speech for each word, you can assign the color green to verbs, red to nouns, blue to adjectives and purple to adverbs. If your word is a verb, you can write the word on an index card in green. When you try to retrieve the visual picture of the word you would then see it as green, meaning it was a verb. If the word was mainly used as a verb, but could also be a noun, you could underline the word in red to indicate its use as a noun.

If you are an auditory learner, saying the words and their definitions aloud will be helpful. Singing the words and creating a rhyme for the definition is another method for the auditory learner.

The kinesthetic student learns best by creating muscle memory through writing the word and its definition several times. To get your vocabulary into your long-term memory, you need to study the words several times over the course of the day and the week. Begin by making index cards with the word on one side and the definition on the opposite side. Review the words daily for a few minutes at each viewing. Before you know it, the words and their definitions will become familiar and only a few words will require more focus to remember.

Some students need to do a little of each method in order for the words to reach their long-term memory. Experiment with different methods until you find the one that works for you.

If you will be tested on all the words in a unit at the end of a unit, continue to review the words in all units each week. Do not wait until just before the test to review previous units. Spending a few minutes each week to review will save you many hours of study before the test and will also relieve tension, thus making you more relaxed. A relaxed student performs better on tests.

I have tried everything you suggested, and I still have homework problems.

You obviously care about succeeding. If you have not been successful using the methods in this book, it is important to never ever give up. I would suggest you talk to your teacher and share all the things you have tried to be successful. Ask him if there is anything else you can try.

You may need a homework coach to talk with daily until you can get on the right track. I am here to help students, so email me (homeworksolutions@hotmail.com). I would love to work with you.

Appendix

Begin today to plan for a brighter future.

Using a daily activity sheet will help you see how you are using your time. It will help you plan more efficiently.

1. Make several copies of this sheet.

2. Record everything you do for the next five days.

3. Highlight all the activities. The blank space will indicate the time you have left to complete homework.

4. At the end of the five days, look at how much time you spent doing non-homework activities. Decide if any of your activities interfere with completing your homework.

• Are there any activities you can eliminate?

• Will you need to do some assignments during lunch or recess or in the car going home to complete all your assignments?

• Are there any activities that attract you and draw your attention away from completing your homework? Can you treat yourself to these activities once you complete all your assignments?

Complete the following task and keep it for your records. Posting it in a visible location will keep it in your memory.

Record your goal. Be sure to be very specific. Example: I am going to keep track of my papers each day.

List what you are going to do to change. Be specific.

Examples:

1. I will place my papers in the front of my homework folder before I leave school.

2. I will do the work and then place the completed work in the back pocket of my homework folder.

3. I will place the folder in my backpack.

4. I will do this every day.

5. I will keep track of my progress every day.

P.M. Daily Activity Log

3:00-3:15

3:15-3:30

3:30-3:45

3:45-4:00

4:00-4:15

4:15-4:30

4:30-4:45

4:45-5:00

5:00-5:15

5:15-5:30

5:30-5:45

5:45-6:00

6:00-6:15

6:15-6:30

6:30-6:45

6:45-7:00

7:00-7:15

7:15-7:30

7:30-7:45

7:45-8:00

8:00-8:15

8:15-8:30

8:30-8:45

Be sure to include eating, brushing your teeth, bathing, eating dinner, walking the dog, skateboarding, playing Nintendo or taking out the trash. Remember to include time for friends and phone calls.

Model
Planning
Steps

Use a calendar to plan long-term projects.

Planning activities backwards has always been helpful. Decide on your due date. List all activities that are to be completed. Some activities may have several steps. Schedule all steps on the planner. Completing the tasks you dislike at the beginning will get them out of the way and leave only those projects you enjoy doing. Using color coding is also helpful.

Black can be used to indicate the due date. Red could indicate the activities that will require the most effort. Green could represent those items that are less urgent. Blue could indicate the least urgent items.

Recording the amount of time you believe each item will take to complete will help you plan effectively.

Book
Report

1. Record the due date of the report, project or presentation in your day planner.

2. Count the number of days until the project is due.

3. Determine the number of days needed to complete the project. Will you need to practice a speech, prepare a poster, build a model or make a diorama?

4. Subtract this number from the total number of days available. This will leave the number of days you have to read the book.

5. Divide the number of pages in your book by the number of available days. Now you know the number of pages you need to read each day to be on target to turn your project in on time.

6. Determine if the number of pages is realistic for you. If it is not, consider finding a shorter book. If you are a slow reader, choosing a book that requires you to read 40 pages a day will be impossible for you to complete. You will be setting yourself up for failure. Choosing a book that requires you to read 12 pages

a day might be more realistic. You will have a better chance of being successful. If you have after-school activities, plan for them by doing extra reading on another night.

7. Keep to your schedule. You might find that once you create the schedule, you complete the task sooner than anticipated. Because you have planned, you <u>will not</u> find yourself finishing the book the night before the report is due.

8. Use "sticky notes" to keep track of important events and characters for your report. When you begin writing your report or presentation, you can utilize the "sticky notes" to organize your writing.

The following page demonstrates how one student created a plan sheet for completing a book report project that required a presentation. You'll note that this student included outside activities on the calendar to be certain he was not overloaded.

Sample Plan for a Monthly Book Report

This plan was created for a 248-page book.

Sunday	Monday	Tuesday	Wednesday	Thursday	Friday	Saturday
			1 Book Report Assigned Due June 3rd	**2** Choose Book Read 10 pages Soccer Practice	**3** Read 20 Pages	**4** Soccer Game Read 16 pages
5 Read 20 Pages	**6** Read 16 pages	**7** Read 16 Pages Soccer	**8** Read 16 pages	**9** Read 16 Pages Soccer	**10** Study for Big Science Test	**11** Campout with Scouts
12 Campout with Scouts Study for Big Science Test	**13** Read 5 Pages Study for Big Science Test	**14** Read 16 Pages Soccer	**15** Study for Big Science Test	**16** Study for Big Science Test Soccer Practice	**17** Read 20 Pages	**18** Soccer Game Read 20 Pages
19 Read 20 Pages	**20** Read 20 Pages	**21** Read 17 pages	**22** Compose Presentation	**23** Ask Teacher to Edit and Review	**24** Obtain Props if necessary and begin practicing the presentation	**25** Practice Presentation
26 Practice Presentation	**27** Practice Presentation	**28** Practice Presentation for an audience	**29** Practice Presentation	**30** Practice Presentation for an audience	**31** Practice Presentation for an audience	

Apr 2002

S	M	T	W	T	F	S
	1	2	3	4	5	6
7	8	9	10	11	12	13
14	15	16	17	18	19	20
21	22	23	24	25	26	27
28	29	30				

Jun 2002

S	M	T	W	T	F	S
						1
2	3	4	5	6	7	8
9	10	11	12	13	14	15
16	17	18	19	20	21	22
23	24	25	26	27	28	29
30						